INTRODUCTION TO ART SONG

BARITONE/BASS

Songs in English for
Classical Voice Students

Compiled by Joan Frey Boytim

ISBN 978-1-4950-6467-8

To access companion recorded piano accompaniments online, visit:
www.halleonard.com/mylibrary

5739-4926-3560-6662

G. SCHIRMER, Inc.

DISTRIBUTED BY
HAL•LEONARD®
CORPORATION
7777 W. BLUEMOUND RD. P.O. BOX 13819 MILWAUKEE, WI 53213

www.musicsalesclassical.com
www.halleonard.com

PREFACE

Introduction to Art Song is intended for any beginning classical singer, teenager through adult. In most studios we have students who remain in traditional voice lessons for any number of years. As teachers, this gives us the time to determine the work ethic, the innate talent, and the personality of the student as we explore repertoire. In addition, we often accept beginning students who, for a number of reasons, will only be in our studios for a year or less. It seemed desirable to develop a book of previously successful, well-liked songs in English which are not particularly difficult, yet more mature than the *Easy Songs for Beginning Singers* series for use with these students.

A teacher browsing through the collections will find many familiar songs, but often in alternate keys from what has been previously published. Very often after recitals students will ask to sing a song they heard another singer perform from *The First Book of Solos* series, but it is not published in a suitable key. Some male voice examples: "When I Think Upon the Maidens," "Brother Will, Brother John," "Give a Man a Horse He Can Ride" and "Shenandoah." Female voice examples are "I Love All Graceful Things," "Danny Boy," "The Green Dog," and "Come to the Fair." In my own teaching some of my students will want to have their voice type appropriate volume of *Introduction to Art Song* for access to songs in comfortable keys.

Songs from American and British composers appear which are not included in previous collections. Of special interest are three, short, early songs by Samuel Barber only recently published: "Longing," "Thy Love" and "Music, When Soft Voices Die."

No sacred songs, Christmas songs or spirituals have been included, which makes the collections practical for use in beginning voice classes. The vocal ranges are moderate and the accompaniments are not extremely difficult. Each volume includes 15 to 20 songs.

This final set of four anthologies completes my various compilations of vocal repertoire books for beginning to intermediate singers, which began in 1991 with *The First Book of Solos*.

I want to thank my inspiring editor, Richard Walters, for believing in me, and offering his fine guidance, patience, friendship, and promoting the 60 published compilations, which I hope have made life easier for teachers all over the world. I also wish to thank Hal Leonard Corporation for giving me this amazing opportunity.

Joan Frey Boytim
compiler

CONTENTS

Pianists on the recordings: [1]Laura Ward, [2]Brendan Fox

The price of this publication includes access to companion recorded accompaniments online,
for download or streaming, using the unique code found on the title page.
Visit www.halleonard.com/mylibrary and enter the access code.

THE BLACK DRESS

Text adapted and Music by
John Jacob Niles

BLACK IS THE COLOR OF MY TRUE LOVE'S HAIR

John Jacob Niles

With great tenderness ♩ = 72

p

Black, black,

black is the col-or of my true love's hair, Her lips _____ are some-thing

ro-sy fair, The ___ pert-est ___ face and the dain-ti-est ___ hands— I

* Troublesome Creek, which empties into the Kentucky River.

Black, black, black is the col-or of my true love's hair, Her lips _____ are some-thing ro-sy fair, The __ pert - est __ face and the dain-ti-est __ hands– I love _____ the grass where-on she stands.

BROTHER WILL, BROTHER JOHN

Elizabeth Charles Welborn

John Sacco

With sly jocularity ♩ = 82

14

Will, Broth-er John, Broth-er Will, Broth-er John, Broth-er

Will, Broth-er John.

f freely
Why mope a-round with fu-ne-re-al fac-es, Whip up your nag and

sfz colla voce

loos-en the trac-es. Take a lit-tle joy, take a lit-tle plea-sure,

a tempo, slyly

a tempo

COME AGAIN, SWEET LOVE

John Dowland

To Daisy
THE DAISIES
from *Three Songs*

James Stephens

Samuel Barber
Op. 2, No. 1

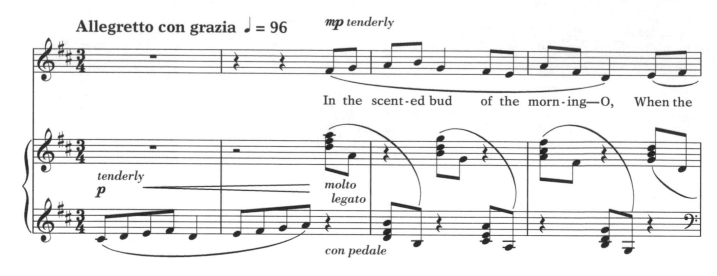

Poem from *Collected Poems of James Stephens.* Printed by permission of The Macmillan Company, publishers.

The Windmill,
Rogers Park
July 20, 1927

*In Stephens' poem the word is "happily," which Barber chose to set on two notes rather than three.

DOWN BY THE SALLY GARDENS

William Butler Yeats

Irish air
arranged by Herbert Hughes

15
leaves grow on the tree, But I be-ing young and

18
fool - ish With her did not a-gree.

22
In a field by the riv - er My love and I did

26
stand, And on my lean-ing shoul - der She

MY LOVELY CELIA

Text by the composer

George Monro

KITTY, MY LOVE, WILL YOU MARRY ME?

Old Ulster Song

Arranged by Herbert Hughes

Allegro
(In lilting fashion)

Kit - ty, my love, will you mar - ry me? Kit - ty, my love, will you go, O!

Kit - ty, my love, will you mar - ry me? Ei - ther say Yes or say No, O!

I ha'e a bal - lad, a bal - lad, It's all a - bout Kit - ty, my dear, An'

I ha'e my gran - ny's oul' cra - dle That she bid me rock in a year, O!

Kit - ty, my love, will you mar - ry me? Kit - ty, my love, will you go, O!

Kit - ty, my love, will you mar - ry me? Ei - ther say Yes or say No, O!

ON RICHMOND HILL THERE LIVES A LASS

(The Lass of Richmond Hill)

James Hook

1. On Rich-mond Hill there lives a lass More bright than May-day
2. Ye Ze-phyrs gay that fan the air And wan-ton thro' the
3. How hap-py will that shep-herd be Who calls this nymph his

morn, _____ Whose charms all oth-er maids sur-pass, A rose with-out a thorn.
grove, _____ Oh whis-per to the charm-ing fair I die for her I love.
own, _____ Oh may her choice be fix'd on me; Mine's fix'd on her a-lone.

SEA FEVER

John Masefield

John Ireland

to Alice Forsythe Mosher

SHOES

Kathleen Lockhart Manning

meet? _____ Was the way bright or was the day cloud - y,

or was there rain and sleet? Or did you take her

where the mead - ows kissed her pass - ing feet?

Tho' you may take her o - ver the high road down to the sing - ing

To A.C. Landsberg

TAKE, O TAKE THOSE LIPS AWAY

from *Five Shakespeare Songs* (Second Set)

William Shakespeare
from *Measure for Measure*

Roger Quilter
Op. 23, No. 4

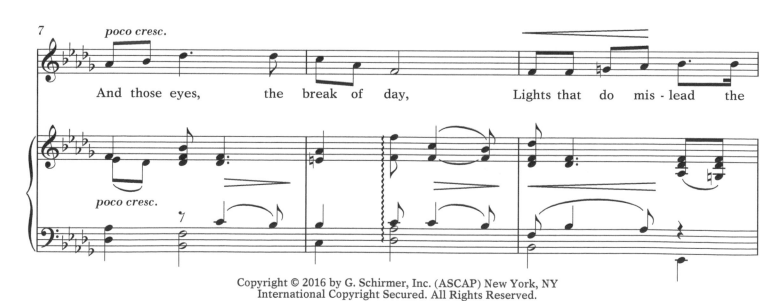

TRADE WINDS

John Masefield

Frederick Keel

With a smooth flowing rhythm

In the

har - bour, in the is - land, in the Span - ish Seas, Are the

ti - ny white hou - ses and the or - ange - trees, And day - long,

tune Of the qui - et voice call - ing me, The

long low croon _ Of the stea - dy trade _ winds blow -

- - - - - - - - - - - ing. _____

To Walter Creighton

UNDER THE GREENWOOD TREE

from *Five Shakespeare Songs* (Second Set)

William Shakespeare
from *As You Like It*

Roger Quilter
Op. 23, No. 2

Un - der the green-wood tree Who loves to lie with me, And

turn his mer - ry note Un - to the sweet bird's throat, Come

48

WHEN I HAVE SUNG MY SONGS

Words and Music by
Ernest Charles

When I have sung my songs to you, _____ I'll sing no more.

'Twould be a sac-ri-lege to sing ___ At an-oth-er door.

WAYFARING STRANGER

Words and Music adapted from
The Original Sacred Harp

Arranged by
John Jacob Niles

I am a poor way-far-ing stran-ger, While jour-n'ying

through this world of woe, Yet there's no sick - ness, toil, nor dan-ger In that fair

To the memory of my friend, Mrs. Cary-Elwes

WEEP YOU NO MORE

from *Seven Elizabethan Songs*

Words Anonymous

Music by
Roger Quilter
Op. 12, No. 1

WHEN I THINK UPON THE MAIDENS

Philip Ashbrooke

Michael Head

game?

Flor - a, O - live, And ___ the oth - ers,

colla voce

How I ha - ted all their broth - ers! Ah ___

cresc.

f *dim.* *mp*

Fic - kle Cu - pid, Fic - kle Cu - pid

p

dim. *p*

you're ___ to ___ blame! ___

pp

Years have passed and yet I'm sin - gle, Torn and un - de - ci - ded still, Cla - ra, Ma - bel, what a vis - ion! I can't come to a de - cis - ion, ___ And I hope I ne - ver will!